SELF CONFIDENCE FOR MANAGERS

SELF CONFIDENCE FOR MANAGERS

Series " Management Skills for Managers "
By: D.K. Hawkins
Version 1.1 ~September 2021
Published by D.K. Hawkins at KDP
Copyright ©2021 by D.K. Hawkins. All rights reserved.

No part of this publication may be reproduced, distributed or transmitted in any form or by any means including photocopying, recording or other electronic or mechanical methods or by any information storage or retrieval system without the prior written permission of the publishers, except in the case of very brief quotations embodied in critical reviews and certain other noncommercial uses permitted by copyright law.

All rights reserved, including the right of reproduction in whole or in part in any form.

All information in this book has been carefully researched and checked for factual accuracy. However, the author and publisher make no warranty, express or implied, that the information contained herein is appropriate for every individual, situation, or purpose and assume no responsibility for errors or omissions.

The reader assumes the risk and full responsibility for all actions. The author will not be held responsible for any loss or damage, whether consequential, incidental, special, or otherwise, that may result from the information presented in this book.

All images are free for use or purchased from stock photo sites or royalty-free for commercial use. I have relied on my own observations as well as many different sources for this book, and I have done my best to check facts and give credit where it is due. In the event that any material is used without proper permission, please contact me so that the oversight can be corrected

The information provided in this book is for informational purposes only and is not intended to be a source of advice or credit analysis with respect to the material presented. The information and/or documents contained in this book do not constitute legal or financial advice and should never be used without first consulting with a financial professional to determine what may be best for your individual needs.

The publisher and the author do not make any guarantee or other promise as to any results that may be obtained from using the content of this book. You should never make any investment decision without first consulting with your own financial advisor and conducting your own research and due diligence. To the maximum extent permitted by law, the publisher and the author disclaim any and all liability in the event any information, commentary, analysis, opinions, advice and/or recommendations contained in this book prove to be inaccurate, incomplete or unreliable, or result in any investment or other losses.

Content contained or made available through this book is not intended to and does not constitute legal advice or investment advice and no attorney-client relationship is formed. The publisher and the author are providing this book and its contents on an "as is" basis. Your use of the information in this book is at your own risk.

TABLE OF CONTENTS.

- TABLE OF CONTENTS. 4
- INTRODUCTION. 5
- CHAPTER 1 10
  - Confidence In Yourself As A Manager And The Workplace. 10
- CHAPTER 2 20
  - Developing A Confident Attitude As A Manager. 20
- CHAPTER 3 29
  - Developing Your Self-Confidence and Intelligence. 29
- CHAPTER 4 34
  - Develop Self-Confidence and Leadership Qualities. 34
- CHAPTER 5 39
  - Empowering Your Self Confidence Building Exercises. 39
- CHAPTER 6 44
  - Leadership Skills Contribute to Self-Confidence and Self-Esteem. 44
- CHAPTER 7 54
  - Self-Confidence Power Lists For Strong Leadership. 54
- CHAPTER 8 59
  - Significant Steps Toward Self-Confidence. 59
- CONCLUSION. 65

INTRODUCTION.

As a manager, your self-esteem and confidence can be the difference between riding the fast track to success and sitting in the sidecar to nowhere.

No matter how good your training, formal education, or tactical talents are if you lack confidence in yourself, you will lack the ability to instill confidence in others. It needs to gain the confidence of others to climb the corporate and business success ladder.

Now for the good news! Self-confidence can be developed in any area of interest. While it may take time, patience, practice, and awareness, people develop confidence daily. Often, we are unaware that we are doing it.

Confidence development is similar to muscular development. You begin cautiously, taking small steps and pushing yourself just a little further each time until you reach your eventual destination of proficiently completing a given task.

If you lack confidence in managing people, the first thing you might want to do is write down where you feel confident and where you don't. Once you've recognized your areas of weakness, write down what it would take for you to feel confident in those areas.

Do you require additional training?

Do you require additional practice?

Is this truly within your skillset?

Once you've determined what you need to do, you can create a strategy to begin getting the skills, tasks, or practice you believe you require. By completing this activity, you will see that there are steps you can take. Nothing is lost, and you are not obligated to suffer, tolerate, or be embarrassed by it.

Having this knowledge will help you increase your self-esteem and confidence. Because, rather than feeling inadequate about yourself and your talents, you will discover that you can improve your performance with your new and unique tools.

Now, plan how you will acquire the new skills and tools you require. Divide things into manageable chunks so that the larger aim does not appear overwhelming. Then create a plan for completing each stage. Each time you take a step, you are strengthening your confidence muscle.

While you work on developing long-lasting confidence in your talents, there are a few simple ways to change your mood, mindset, and inner sentiments of confidence.

If you're working on a presentation or project, allow yourself extra time to prepare. Understanding the content, you're presenting, or the specifics of a project you're working on immediately boosts your self-esteem, confidence, and expertise. This will manifest itself in your interactions with your team and managers.

Concentrate on your progress. Make a list of all the things you've completed at work over the last 90 days, as well as the past year. Make a note next to each accomplishment for which you are genuinely proud. Take note of any positive remarks or expressions of thanks by your teammates or supervisors regarding those accomplishments.

Also, jot down any activities in which you felt insufficient. Consider what you could do, learn or adjust the next time to elicit a favorable or favorable response. It's beneficial to have areas where you can improve! It enables you to continue growing and excelling.

Remember that confidence is your trust in your final potential to execute a specific activity. Therefore, begin gradually raising the bar for yourself. Enroll in a course that will teach you how to perform a new task related to your professional role.

Inquire about the possibility of serving as a professional mentor to someone in need of your expertise. All these actions will increase your confidence, demonstrate your abilities and teach you new skills. True life fulfillment begins with self-esteem and confidence development. You can create the life, career, and dreams of your dreams as a manager.

Are you ready? Let's get started

CHAPTER 1

Confidence In Yourself As A Manager And The Workplace.

Self-confidence occupies the precarious zone between damaged self-esteem and an arrogant ego - Your self-confidence matters. Years of experience have shown me that successful people think that the explicit positive acts, behaviors, and results of individuals they have worked or witnessed have considerably boosted their self-confidence.

If this is true, then we have an obligation as managers to control our self-confidence levels and, more importantly, to inspire others to do the same. According to my experience, many people lack the self-confidence necessary for a successful attitude.

Indeed, they are far more delicate than we may believe. This is an attitude of "can't do" rather than "can do," and it is sadly ingrained by far more negative than positive influences.

I would argue that a healthy sense of self-confidence is a necessary component of performance and success. Self-confidence is commonly defined as a mental state in which one is self-assured about any current thinking or situation. It could be characterized as an emotional state of mind or a belief in one's success ability.

Individuals with self-confidence can exert control over conditions or circumstances rather than being governed by them. As a result, it may aid in the alleviation of anxiety or unwarranted and undesirable concerns. More importantly, it can help to create clear expectations for favorable outcomes.

I propose the following thought: self-confidence is acquired. Your self-confidence is uniquely yours. You should safeguard it and continue to build on it, even if it means having a face-to-face conversation with your reflection in the mirror. I would never promise that it will not experience periods of intense pressure, but the ability to control it is within you.

Indeed, you may learn to leverage your self-confidence to outperform those around you. Believing in oneself gives you an advantage over those who cannot model those same positive thoughts.

This means that you may feel in control in any scenario, regardless of who is around you. Of course, this requires you to be willing to make all necessary efforts to accomplish the task at hand.

Your self-esteem is the bedrock of both personal and professional success. Never allow somebody to take away your self-confidence. It is yours to treasure and cherishes in perpetuity, and only you can allow people to undermine your self-confidence.

Individuals exist at all levels of an organization. Only societal rules, experience, and corporate governance have conferred special privileges on particular persons, such as privileged information, titles, corner offices, and executive perks.

As a result, some have gained real or perceived influence or a position of authority or, more, they have been endowed with the knowledge or power that you or they believe gives them authority over you. The reality is that they entered the world identically and will exit identically - with a first and final breath.

What individuals have been exposed to and learned and how they choose to use what they have learned will determine their position with others. Indeed, regardless of stature, function, or title, I know I have observed and experienced both high and low levels of self-confidence.

I had the opportunity to develop a personal relationship with the company's president very early in my career. On one occasion, I was out canoeing with him on a lake near his summer residence. I was attempting to be quite precise in all of my efforts.

My conversation was stiff and uneasy, consisting primarily of "Yes sir, no sir, three bags full sir." He tipped me into the lake as we approached the dock, and he stepped out of the canoe. With a pleasant smile, he offered his hand to assist me out of the water and casually reminded me that he, like everyone else, enjoyed having fun.

I'll never forget that lesson; that talk implanted in me a sense of self-confidence that lasted for the rest of my years. I learned how to interact with people who were older than me. While I treat employees with the respect they deserve or have earned, the reality is that they are just like you and me.

Each of us deserves and should earn an appropriate level of personal respect. Consider how your interactions and observations with others while on your path to success may significantly impact your learning and the development of your self-confidence.

Managing Upward.

Your better self-confidence will be crucial when interacting with more senior individuals. They will soon perceive it, feel more comfortable around you, and respect your capabilities regardless of the circumstances. It is possible that the leaders themselves are uncertain or lacking in understanding on some subjects.

As predicted, managers cannot be expected to be specialists in every field. Your self-esteem will enable continuous dependence on you. They will develop an appreciation for you as a result of the value you contribute to the workplace.

You may notice that as their faith in you grows, they will likely delegate additional responsibilities to you. They may not always accurately detect or appraise your skills or personal motivation for a given work. As a result, you'll need to communicate this to them to finish the task properly.

Managing up is an important skill to develop when you uncover your true certainty and understanding. This self-assurance will manifest itself within you. Indeed, it may be the deciding factor in your success.

Simultaneously, it might position you as a role model for other employees looking to advance their careers.

Many times, I have attempted to manage up or serve as a coach for my employees. For instance, I've offered them pointers on how to do things better or suggested alternatives that have worked effectively in previous similar instances.

One of the simplest ways to proceed is to inquire about their feelings about how things transpired or how they would have done something differently. Occasionally, I would come out and ask if they are open to a different approach and leave them with appealing options to select from. With time and the appropriate level of respect, leaders will often seek you out - a tremendously rewarding experience.

Managing Downward.

As you interact with your employees, your self-confidence will serve as a beacon for their unwavering trust in you as a manager; as your confidence in a particular subject grows, theirs will as well. Allow it to lapse, and you will be scrutinized.

Allowing and encouraging your employees to bring forth ideas - particularly those that are superior to your own. Please encourage them to do their best and be open to possibly some will eventually advance quicker than you.

Encouraging this behavior teaches kids that they, too, can achieve more success than they ever imagined. Also, they will admire you for promoting this approach. Not attempt to assume or interpret what individuals want, as this will close them off to a world they are unaware exists.

As a manager, it is your responsibility to foster an open workplace and guide exploring the world at your fingertips. What occurs as a result? You have confidence in them, they have confidence in you, and they have confidence in themselves. You have generated powerful energy that will catalyze their and your success!

Managing Across.

The same principles apply when managing your peers as they do, whether managing upwards or below. You will be scrutinized and observed. The climate is both collaborative and competitive, and the individual with the most self-confidence will often stride further than their friends.

Acquire information or facts, assess the problem realistically, create acceptable goals for yourself and others and solicit the assistance of people who can favorably affect the outcome.

A confident leadership team will determine the culture of an organization, a culture of self-confidence! This is a culture that inquires more than it instructs and rewards more than it punishes.

When you learn to embrace and utilize your level of self-confidence, it may be a tremendous instrument for pushing you toward your personal and professional goals. However, a word of caution: avoid conflating unbridled ego with controlled or perceived self-confidence in yourself and others.

I've discovered firsthand that a manager's self-assurance should be developed in two complementary ways: maintaining and strengthening one's confidence and eliciting it in those they lead. Leadership success at the managerial level should not be determined just by the leader but by the confidence of those to whom the leader is accountable.

CHAPTER 2

Developing A Confident Attitude As A Manager.

Have you noticed that the most successful managers communicate, think and behave differently than you do? Have you ever watched Oprah on her television show and thought to yourself, "What a wonderful attitude!" How am I to emulate him/her?

Fantastic news! You, too, can be like these people. How do you accomplish this? By changing your views and behaviors. The great news is that each of us can change, and we can begin changing at any time, for example, RIGHT NOW.

The good news is that it is OUR RESPONSIBILITY. Nobody else is impeding us. Thus, the flushing noise you hear now is all of our justifications for "why things are the way they are."

How do you change your perceptions?

That is accomplished through different distinct beliefs about yourself and your situation. This requires intentional effort at first. All the tactics discussed in this chapter aim to increase one's sense of self-confidence as a manager.

The other component is changing your behavior. If your current actions have not resulted in the success, you desire. However, you define success personally and distinctively; you must act differently. As Albert Einstein put it, "insanity is repeating the same action and expecting a different outcome."

A new you emerges when diverse attitudes and actions are combined: more powerful, calmer, and loving. Also, your views and behaviors are inextricably linked. Once one of them is changed, the other will follow.

There is considerable strength in action. Success and all accompanying sensations will follow if you take the appropriate actions. As you develop a more self-confident mindset, you will continually feel unstoppable, which will motivate you to action because you understand what to do and are confident in your ability to do it.

Whether you begin by focusing on attitudes or actions, you will eventually find yourself on a path that includes establishing a successful mindset and effective ways of acting. All of this - the attitudes and talents - eventually become absorbed and develop a new way of being. It's simple.

Here are few strategies to assist you in developing a successful and self-confident mindset.

For one week, begin each workday with one of the three approaches listed above. Before you do anything else, read your WHY narrative to yourself or close your eyes and imagine yourself as the king or close your eyes and imagine how your hero would tackle the day.

If you're unsure how to go or feel down throughout the day, take a break and experiment with another strategy.

1. Construct your own WHY narrative.

Remind yourself why this is the correct concept (e.g., being a team leader or pursuing a large company objective), why you are the appropriate person to execute it, and why now is the ideal moment. Retell that narrative to yourself repeatedly. If you enjoy listening to knowledge, record yourself telling the narrative and listen to it whenever you need to.

Reminding yourself of your tale helps you develop self-confidence, as we often focus on the disconnects or flaws in our narratives. "I began studying business in college but was never particularly fond of it. I took a job in sales but despised my supervisor and the way he pressed us for sales. Now I'm attempting direct sales, and who knows whether it will succeed!"

In your story, search for your genuine abilities and desires. Then look at the many ways they have manifested themselves throughout your life. You may have always had a natural ability to assist others, put them at ease, or educate them. You might excel at fashion and design, technology, or creating a lovely home.

It reminds me of my unique blend of qualities (including tenacity and a passion for learning) and experiences (including founding two businesses and growing them to over $1 million in revenue) and how they have molded me and equipped me with a gift that I am now sharing with others.

2. Visualize the king.

Consider yourself to be the kingdom's compassionate and absolute monarch. Individuals adore and admire you. You possess complete authority, as seen by the crown you wear and the golden staff you wield.

Consider wearing the crown, holding your staff, approaching the throne, and taking a seat. Following that, a senior official enters to ask you the question you've been thinking about. What are your feelings?

What is your response?

3. What would your hero do in this situation?

Choose someone you admire greatly: Oprah, the CEO of your firm, your spiritual role model. What, if they were in your shoes, would they do? It's strange how often you'll be at a loss for what to do, but you'll know what your hero would do!

4. Assemble a support system.

Alecia Huck, a motivational speaker, adds a wrinkle to this. She has conditioned her girlfriends so that when she calls in a bad mood, they instantly begin reminding her of how wonderful she is, and it's always effective because she provided them with the script to follow!

In general, your employees will understand how prepared you are for the task at hand. They can serve as a reminder that you are doing the right thing, doing it well, and making a difference.

One significant caveat to hiring family and friends: you must avoid naysayers. When you change your life, other people may feel intimidated, either because they fear it will break their existing relationship with you or because they are projecting their anxieties onto you. Regrettably, some of your family members may be doubters.

If they are cannot assist you, they must at the very least remain impartial. If they are cannot stay neutral, you may need to avoid discussing the subject entirely.

5. Act.

Remember that attitude and behaviors are inextricably linked; one influences the other. Whatever your current state of mind, you will feel better after you take action. I am a firm believer in the efficacy of an optimistic outlook, and occasionally, it is not present.

During those times, regardless of how you feel, you need to take the next step and the next. After you've taken action (and walked away from your work, called a friend, had a glass of wine, and gotten a good night's sleep), you'll have a new perspective.

A significant portion of your success will be determined by your ability to manage your attitudes. Self-confidence combined with action will go you a long way on the path to success.

When next year arrives, you can look forward to celebrating your recent accomplishments, exuding confidence and comfort, and donning a fabulous pair of shoes. You can begin your journey immediately.

The first step is simple - all you have to do is think differently and behave differently. It's entirely up to you and your mentality.

Awakening.

Use one of the first three procedures daily for the next seven days. At the end of the week, assess whether these approaches improved your ability to navigate your day. Did you gain confidence in your interactions with others? Was it easy to choose a focal point?

CHAPTER 3

Developing Your Self-Confidence and Intelligence.

The guidance of your unconscious mind, which generates your dreams, will assist you in developing your self-confidence and wisdom as a manager. You will learn to avoid making mistakes and always to do what is necessary to achieve in life.

The evolution of your personality will determine your self-esteem. Your psychological metamorphosis will be determined by the knowledge gained through unconscious learning. These courses will teach you how to manage your behavior. Always act after considering all of your available options in every situation.

Your vision will assist you in developing confidence in your abilities. You can forecast the future and identify any potential threats, errors, or other negative aspects that could result in future issues. This way, you'll be able to remedy any errors and set the stage for the positive future outcomes you wish.

This potential will increase your sense of security and provide you with the courage to tackle life's hardships. You will sincerely believe that you can resolve all issues, surmounting all hurdles and ultimately triumphing.

Only when you believe in your inner strength can you develop self-confidence. However, to believe in your inner strength, you must eradicate erroneous notions and behavioral irregularities that keep you from feeling strong.

I simplified Carl Jung's dream interpretation approach for you, but it took two decades to translate innumerable dreams into practice and heal many patients through dream therapy. You are fortunate because, as a result of my discoveries, I could simplify the dream language and the process of transformation through dream therapy.

Carl Jung could not see the entirety of the human psyche's content since he halted his studies at a particular point, admitting ignorance from that point forward. I continued his investigation, revealing what he couldn't see with his limited understanding.

As a result, I'm going to state plainly that you've inherited a ridiculous wild conscience that desires to destroy your human conscience through crazy and exert control over your actions.

All of your dreams are essentially a defense mechanism against your primal conscience, the anti-conscience, which is responsible for developing mental diseases within your human conscience.

Native Americans and many people associated with ancient civilizations used to regard the interpretation of dreams as sacred. However, many barbarian societies equipped with formidable weapons and armies succeeded in destroying peaceful societies that emphasized the significance of dreams and life.

Today, most people feel that dreams are meaningless or are reflections of our emotions and worries. This impression is entirely false. Carl Jung's discoveries regarding the meaning of dreams and my discoveries due to continuing his research have put an end to all preconceived notions about the meaning and significance of dreams.

Unfortunately, the dreadful competition that characterizes our contemporary violent and greed-based civilization prohibits people from finding salvation. Many significant scientific discoveries continue to be overlooked by the world because many prominent scientists, marketers, and other professionals fear losing their privileges.

These specialists are unconcerned with averting global misery just since fresh, new beneficial solutions have been discovered. They would rather keep humanity from discovering the truth to maintain their social standing. As a result, they make a substantial effort to outperform their opponents.

This is why, to this day, the world has largely overlooked the amazing findings of psychiatrist Carl Jung, even though his method of dream interpretation is so beneficial that it must be taught in schools.

Native Americans and many ancient civilizations that saw dreams as sacred were entirely correct. Dreams are important because they convey invaluable messages from the intelligent unconscious mind. The unconscious mind is divine in origin; it functions similarly to a very generous natural physician.

You must begin developing your self-confidence by eradicating the impediments to your progress. Then you must cultivate your intelligence. Your psychological transformation and behavioral health will result in increased self-confidence.

This is why it will always define your personality; it will not vanish due to life's struggles. Your self-confidence will always be present, assisting you in always triumphing and shining.

CHAPTER 4

Develop Self-Confidence and Leadership Qualities.

Develop your self-confidence if you want to advance as a manager in your organization, as it is one of the most important leadership characteristics. In this chapter, I discuss tips that can help anyone improve leadership behavior at the managerial level.

Without self-confidence, you'll have a difficult time securing a position of leadership. To begin, you must understand that leadership attributes are behavior-based.

All outstanding managers earn the trust and admiration of those with whom they come into touch. On the other hand, effective managers rely more on their abilities than on their leadership. Managers place a higher premium on communication organization and scheduling than true leaders do.

Please do not believe that those skills are unimportant leadership characteristics, as they are essential in leadership. However, true leadership conduct is considerably more dependent on personality than on basic managerial abilities.

Some individuals naturally develop leadership characteristics as a result of the positive upbringing they got. However, the average person on the street does not aim to be a leader and hence does not require the self-confidence required by a true leader.

Construct Self-Confidence.

Your leadership style is determined by personality characteristics such as:

Humility, Integrity, Honesty, Sincerity, Commitment, Wisdom, Courage, Compassion, Self-confidence, an Optimistic Attitude, Sensitivity, Determination, and Passion for your efforts. Also, if you wish to be a leader in your firm, you must first cultivate leadership behavior in your thinking.

Dress for Success is a general rule.

Whether you are a man or a woman, your clothes tell volumes about you. Thus, you must spend money on clothing to earn money as a leader.

This tip concerning external appearance is one of the simplest ways to create all leadership traits. It is not primarily about leadership conduct, which is not physical; instead, it is spiritual. You can steal a leader's clothes but not their leadership behavior.

Gentlemen, you should learn to tie your 1own ties. Clip-on ties are obnoxious. You never know when you're going to have to untie your tie. Consider the following scenario: you're in a lengthy business meeting. Also, a hand-tied tie looks great.

Ladies, a hairstylist can make a world of difference in how you look and feel. Consider getting a new haircut and dressing for success. You'll feel better about yourself and gain self-confidence as a result.

Consider enrolling in a public speaking course.

I'll begin by focusing on the first behavioral leadership skill I'll discuss, public speaking. While you may be the most qualified employee in the organization to lead the conversation, having public speaking experience, which you can obtain in college, can help you stand comfortably in front of an audience.

Public speaking is a skill that can be honed. Guiding concepts and effective public speaking methods, which you can learn in a public speaking school, can help you improve your leadership behavior and boost your confidence.

Take a class in Speech Communication as soon as possible. Choose one that focuses on public speaking since it may help you conquer your fear of public speaking. It may help you develop self-confidence and give you the certainty that people will genuinely listen to your message rather than assessing your speaking style when you present a speech.

Assume You Already Have Self-confidence.

You do not have to be an actor to begin, and if you are extremely insecure, you can even start by play-acting in private. It will assist you in developing self-confidence.

You may develop the self-confidence that you are capable of creating, but you must work at it. You can overcome insecurities that are buried deep inside your subconscious mind and may be preventing you from reaching your full potential.

CHAPTER 5

Empowering Your Self Confidence Building Exercises.

Self-confidence is to believe in what you can accomplish. It is sometimes interchanged with self-esteem; yet, they are significantly different from one other.

You lack self-confidence if you often doubt your talents. If you are having issues developing your self-confidence, you might need to try practicing some confidence-building activities.

The Two-Minute Confidence Building Exercises

Time is not a hurdle in building your self-confidence. If you are often occupied by stuff, you may attempt the two-minute confidence-boosting exercises:

Face the mirror and picture your reflection as a different person. Pretend that you will be interacting with that person.

Focus and attempt to keep your head motionless. A Tai Chi visualization strategy can be of good help when it comes to this. It is just imagining that a string is hanging your head. Maintaining a level head is important during this workout. With your head and neck adjusted, you are free of tension and stress.

Begin convincing yourself that you are a role model for confidence. You may need to refocus your attention on your desired state. For instance, suppose you are a medical student. Consider yourself a doctor.

Take a deep breath every now and while facing the mirror. Believe that your room is well ventilated and that you are surrounded by plenty of fresh air —- savor it. As you inhale and exhale, allow yourself to feel that the fresh air is filling your entire system.

Empty your mind of stressful thoughts during this procedure and convince yourself that each time you exhale, you are also letting go of these thoughts. You will notice that the air permeates every cell in your body and that any sense of anxiousness will go, replaced by a sense of tranquility.

This remark may be of assistance to you: "I am capable of accomplishing this! Everything will finally fall into place in my favor." You are not required to repeat the stated statement; instead, you may say anything positive to yourself.

Positivity is among the keys to a fulfilling existence. A positive thought is powerful, and its importance cannot be overstated. Positive-minute confidence-building practice

You can surely do it whenever you need a boost of confidence. If you are a busy person, you can incorporate this into your daily routine, preferably before leaving the house, to reclaim pleasant energies.

Additional Confidence-Building Activities.

Each of us had had days when the globe did not appear to rotate in the way it should, and the storm did not appear to diminish. Apart from the two-minute confidence-building practice, there are a few other ways to improve your confidence. Here are a few examples:

Find a physical activity that you enjoy. Exercise, whether aerobics, stretching, jogging, or cycling, is a way to boost your confidence. Suppose you're feeling down; set aside at least 15 minutes to work through your issues. Regular exercise helps you sleep better and relaxes your stiff muscles. It has been shown to alleviate symptoms of stress and anxiety. As a result, exercise not only improves your appearance it also improves your mood.

Apart from exercising, you might participate in sports. Whether it's volleyball, basketball, baseball, or football, participating in a sport is one of the countless confidence-building exercises you can do. A sport is an excellent way to improve confidence, as hitting or tossing the ball relieves stress.

Take care of yourself. It's acceptable to spend a small portion of your money on yourself. While it is essential to stretch your money, you should allow yourself to enjoy luxury, if only for a day.

Essentially anything! You may purchase new clothing, books, or gadgets for yourself. If you're not interested in material possessions, you can dine at your favorite restaurant or watch a movie.

You are merely shown the route; the remainder is entirely up to you. If you take action, you will discover that everything is manageable. If you take it for granted, you will find yourself at a disadvantage.

CHAPTER 6

Leadership Skills Contribute to Self-Confidence and Self-Esteem.

Business success often hinges on how you utilize leadership abilities as a manager efficiently. This advice column has various recommendations meant to assist you in developing self-confidence and esteem.

Employing leadership qualities in the workplace may well help you earn financial incentives from your employer. Promotional success is contingent upon it, as is the financial success of your business.

Leadership abilities are characterized by action. In other words, it is not a managerial competence in the traditional sense of organizing, scheduling, and the like. On the other side, leadership skills are those that you use to earn the trust, respect, and admiration of others who look up to you, but managerial abilities are also necessary.

Develop self-esteem and confidence, both of which are essential leadership skills. Many people believe poise is an impossible objective. In a moment, I'll discuss how to implement self-improvement and confidence-building practices that helped me; but first, allow me to tell you a true story.

I experienced childhood traumas that impacted my performance and capacity to get work. As a result of my fears, I never had an opportunity to develop into a leader for any organization.

I was raised without parents, and my guardians tortured and neglected me; I left the orphanage where I was reared from the age of five till I graduated from high school with significant emotional wounds.

I hid those terrible recollections from my conscious mind; but, my subconscious mind undermined my conscious memory, shattering my ambition to have a useful life. However, I discovered a strategy for developing self-confidence and self-esteem; this method assisted me in achieving financial success in my life.

I gained the self-control necessary for sales success. Then I was offered the position of district sales manager for Oregon and southern Washington. I developed an unchanging sense of self-worth and confidence, which are essential leadership skills.

Establish goals.

Create self-confidence and self-esteem goals for yourself. It will assist you in believing in yourself. Develop self-confidence and self-esteem, as it is much easy than you may believe.

Make your aims specific.

Quantify your financial achievement. When developing your confidence-building strategies, create a plan of action so that you can track your progress toward any particular goal. You'll find it much simpler to build self-confidence, and you'll gain confidence once you've accomplished a couple of your small goals, which should be very straightforward to achieve.

Make your objectives gradual.

Recognize and understand that you cannot become president of any organization overnight—unless your father owns the business. All that is required is to wait for him to retire. However, if your future map is already etched in rock, you are unlikely to be reading this post.

Setting minor goals makes it easier to develop self-confidence. Your initial objective may be to facilitate a departmental meeting through the delivery of a presentation. You'll gain confidence as you accomplish each of your minor goals.

Make eye contact with others when conversing.

Another essential interpersonal skill that will assist you in developing self-confidence and self-esteem is maintaining eye contact with the person with whom you are conversing. The ability to facilitate dialogue is an important leadership attribute.

When conversing with another individual, take the time to listen to them.

Remember the point I'm making: dialogue is a two-way street. Therefore, bear this quote in mind.

Be an attentive listener. Allow the individual with whom you are conversing adequate time to express their thoughts. By listening, you'll cultivate an aura of warmth. Others will like your company and gain popularity due to acquiring this important interpersonal skill. The end outcome of honing your interpersonal abilities will be an increase in your self-confidence.

Many people feel extremely vulnerable, believing they will never be excellent at anything. This type of poor self-esteem will inevitably result in a loss of confidence in whatever you do throughout your life.

Consider the following: If you have never attempted something, you can never assert that you will fail. For instance, your manager suggests that you supervise a team, but you're afraid you'll ruin it. This type of fear will almost probably keep a person from accepting the job.

However, if you are confident, you would not hesitate to change and willingly accept that task. Inadequate self-confidence might have a detrimental effect on your job progress.
Motivate yourself.

Whether it's a demonstration, a job interview, or anything else, demonstrate to yourself that you're capable. Encourage yourself daily, and you will soon notice your self-confidence rising.

A simple way to encourage oneself is to keep a running list of at least five things you did well that day. This particular practice supports your unshakable belief that you are capable of achieving whatever you set your mind to.

Engage in positive self-talk.

Utilize optimistic self-talk as a means of displacing bad notions that are clogging your mind. Whenever you are tempted by pessimism, remind yourself to "pause" and replace all of them with positive ones.

If you notice yourself striving for perfection, encourage yourself to do your best. For instance, if your mind is filled with depressing thoughts, replace them with happy memories. This tends to make you much more forgiving of yourself; at the same time, continue to strive for improvement.

One excellent technique to overcome pessimism is just to read and hear optimistic things. Reading and listening to positive and affirming items can undoubtedly help you develop your capacities and skills for self-confidence.

Read and listen to stories about prosperous people. You'll notice that most of these people encountered difficult circumstances; they encountered many problems and obstacles in daily life, but they overcame these obstacles and grew to be successful in their endeavors. This method will undoubtedly pay off in the long run, as these become sources of hopeful awareness in your mind.

Visualize your long-term success.

Often visualize yourself rejoicing in success! Feel the genuine delight, expectation, adrenaline, and buzz associated with success. To increase your optimism, visualize yourself as a confident guy or lady. Consider confronting a challenging challenge and triumphing over it with composure and confidence.

Utilize your five sensory faculties to create an intense and realistic image in your mind. Assume you're about to perform your piano concert and are having problems relaxing.

Consider yourself boldly striding to the piano on stage. Consider yourself playing with complete assurance and pleasure. Consider people clapping their hands and shouting "Encore!" Take in the sight, smell, and taste of accomplishment. Isn't it energizing?

Acknowledge your accomplishments.

Give yourself credit for any endeavors you make. Instead of focusing exclusively on success, as a result, emphasize the entire process of attainment, those courageous and straightforward efforts made.

Congratulate and reward yourself whenever you do anything that makes you happy. Allow yourself a break by visiting a restaurant, a decent health spa, or taking the remainder of the day off.

Cultivate these sensations by recalling earlier accomplishments. In your journal, record the instances when you truly feel delighted. It may be an occasion or performance for which you felt both thankfulness and a great sense of accomplishment.

Take comfort in those memories and draw power from them. Declare aloud, "If I was able to accomplish these in the past, I am confident that I can accomplish more in the present and future."

Utilize your leadership abilities because they may assist you in achieving success in all of your activities. Also, it may pave the way for leadership success.

CHAPTER 7

Self-Confidence Power Lists For Strong Leadership.

Most managers underestimate their abilities. Because errors, deficits, and failures often mar the task of motivating individuals to perform at their best

I once knew a woman who earned a master's degree in English from a prestigious university. She adored novels and poetry, and we regularly conversed about them. She often expressed a desire to publish a novel someday. I urged her to begin by writing a narrative one day.

To my astonishment, she voiced reservation, stating that she was not prepared to give it a try. I was perplexed by her attitude, given she was a literature student and a thoughtful, insightful individual. I'd seen samples of her work. It was quite exquisite - significantly more so than the ordinary. She believed she was incapable of doing so. As a result, she never did.

By contrast, our organization previously employed a young computer programmer who insisted that our newly developed web-based application requires a content management system.

I was aware that he lacked experience with this type of programming. Still, he said he could design a generic, self-customizable content management system that would become a stand-alone product.

As a result, we assigned him the project. He made many errors along the road, but it was incredible to watch him grow, and, in the end, he performed what he said he would do, even though he had never done anything similar before.

The distinction between these two individuals is self-confidence, the belief in one's capacity to complete a difficult task.

So, whom would you back to succeed?

The exceptionally gifted individual who believes she is incapable? Or the individual who lacks expertise but is confident he can?

Believe that you can or that you cannot. In either case, you will demonstrate your correctness.

When confronted with the difficulties of leadership, it's natural to doubt oneself. You are aware of your strengths and have accomplished many goals during your life. However, you are aware that you cannot excel in everything. You may believe it is reckless to disregard your limitations.

Do not undervalue yourself! You have a creative mind. You possess vitality. You can build on what you know, gaining knowledge along the way. You can labor diligently and refuse to give up. As the German poet Goethe put it, "Begin whatever you can achieve or envisage; audacity contains brilliance, strength, and magic."

Create the three power lists of a self-confident manager to assist you in becoming an influential leader.

1. Create a list of all your accomplishments - everything you've ever done that you're proud of. Allow yourself time. Commence with your youth. You'll likely discover that you've forgotten about a good deal of your successes!

Each time you catch yourself thinking, "Oh well, that's not much of an accomplishment," push this notion to the back of your mind and record it regardless. Once you're some, the list is complete; go over it slowly. As you analyze each item, express your gratitude and explain why you're delighted with it. This should be done for every success, without exception.

2. Following that, create a list of your knowledge and abilities. Include everything once more. The list will be considerably longer than you anticipated.

3. Finally, create a list of your most endearing characteristics and characteristics. Not attempt modesty!

4. Once you've completed the three lists, repeat to yourself: "In many aspects, I am a strong candidate for leadership. I've learned and accomplished a lot in my life. I am capable of practically everything I set my mind to." Each day, repeat these sentences three times.

It's easy to lose sight of your potential. The three lists provide a thorough examination of your true talents. Create all three and keep them on hand for future use.

You have already earned the right to be self-assured and strong to lead. Recognizing your abilities and accomplishments is analogous to depositing money in a bank. You will not be interested if you devalue the positive aspects of life or neglect to give yourself credit.

Expect great things of yourself, and you'll discover that accomplishing them becomes easier.

CHAPTER 8

Significant Steps Toward Self-Confidence.

Whether you admit it or not, you must have experienced a period of emotional turmoil that nearly destroyed your self-confidence. What sets you apart from the rest is how you handled and managed the circumstance at the time.

If you made it out of the lonely scenario unscathed, you did well. However, if you were among the many who could not recover from such an experience, your self-esteem may have been shattered.

What does this imply? This suggests your faith in your talents has taken a significant hit. You may have felt that you are incapable of doing anything and that making any endeavor would be futile.

So, how do you overcome this perplexing situation?

How can you persuade yourself that you still have a chance at life and the potential to affect change?

The good news is that there are strategies for increasing self-confidence. It might take a while to complete, but it will aid in developing one's self-image. Self-esteem does not develop overnight; it takes time, dedication, and determination.

To develop self-esteem, you must first recognize yourself as the master of your own life and make a secret vow to take every moment as an opportunity to improve.

Take the three important stages for developing self-confidence and determining your true worth.
Step 1: Adopt the Correct Mentality. Do you know how it feels when you're assigned a task but are cannot do it despite your best efforts? It's distressing and irritating, all the more so when you know, you're

devoting all your time and talent to the effort. The issue might be traced back to not having the proper mindset before beginning the assignment.

The same is true when it comes to developing your self-esteem. Before you begin implementing the many tactics or approaches that may assist you in regaining your confidence in yourself, you should mentally prepare for the lengthy trip.

You must take a step back and examine your situation honestly - where you are and where you want to go - then create realistic goals and commit to accomplishing them.

Consider the following five points to assist you in developing the proper mindset:

List Your Ten Significant Achievements. By compiling this list, you are reminding yourself of the accomplishments you have made while your confidence has not yet been shattered. The list could contain something as easy as passing an exam to obtain a driver's license or contributing to community relief operations. You should have a copy of this list on hand to review from time to time.

Emphasize Your Strengths. You can conduct this activity by inquiring your close friends about their perceptions of your strengths and faults. By being aware of these, you will better deal with the opportunities and threats that may present themselves.

Establish Reasonable Goals. Your objectives should be realistic and within your ability. Aim for something that is within your capabilities. This is possible once you have established your trust in your abilities.

Control Your Mind. At this point, you should be able to shut down your mind from negative thoughts that might undermine your confidence. You should develop the ability to disregard negativity and focus on the positive.

Step 1: Make a Public Proclamation of your Commitment. This is crucial - you must make a sincere promise to see the process through from start to finish.

Step 2: Begin the Procedure. Once you've established the proper mindset, you're ready to take the first step and begin the process. It's crucial to remember that you can begin with little steps and should not feel discouraged. Once your confidence in yourself has been rebuilt, you can take on more challenges than you believe your abilities are capable of handling.

Step 3. Accept All Obstacles. Through this approach, you will be able to gradually increase your self-esteem, regardless of how minor the outcomes appear.

With these minor triumphs under your belt, you'll be able to position yourself to accept more significant challenges. When you take on new and more significant difficulties, you effectively communicate that you possess the talents and confidence to overcome them.

Confidence is derived from self-dominion. By adopting the appropriate behaviors, you can bolster your self-esteem, and having healthy self-esteem directly affects your life and all you wish to do.

CONCLUSION.

Self-confident managers have an uncanny ability to attract others to themselves. Subordinates have been found to function efficiently under the direction of confident decision-makers.

Without the attribute, any business's internal system deteriorates, and employees begin to question the management. As a result, workplace rivalry is fostered, and a valuable human resource is lost.

It is assumed that a self-confident individual is knowledgeable about everything. This statement is not accurate. Because self-assured leaders boost people up, they inspire employees to excel as their strength assists others in achieving achievement.

It is stated that confidence cannot be developed overnight. However, this does not mean there is no possibility to improve it. It's a gradual process of education that begins with shifting one's mindset and gaining a new perspective on life.

Recognize your accomplishments as a first step. Concentrate on your professional accomplishments to date rather than obsessing over past failures. Cribbing will make you unhappy.

There is nothing wrong with occasionally patting oneself on the back. It assists in the development of self-esteem. Never underestimate yourself or the effort it took to get to this point.

The second stage is to evaluate your strengths. Where in your personal and professional life do you shine? Naturally, there is always an opportunity for improvement. However, concentrating on your flaws will not improve matters either.

Your life should be centered on your strengths. Begin to believe in yourself. Allow your day's minor frustrations and disappointments to outweigh all of your spectacular successes.

Consider your plans. What do you envision yourself doing in the next five years?

What do you need to do, and how do you get there?

Acquire the ability to control it. Mark Victor Hansen stated: "Wait until everything is perfect before proceeding. It will never be without flaws. There will always be barriers, difficulties, and less-than-ideal conditions.

What is the point? Get started immediately. With each step, you will become stronger, more skilled, more confident, and more successful."

Management Skills for Managers

1. Time Management for Managers
2. Employee Coaching for Managers
3. Team Building for Managers
4. Self Confidence for Managers
5. Negotiation Skills for Managers
6. Customer Service Skills for Managers
7. Coming soon

www.ingramcontent.com/pod-product-compliance
Lightning Source LLC
Chambersburg PA
CBHW070127230526
45472CB00004B/1459